Hearing Still

Also by George Messo:

Poetry
From the Pine Observatory (2000)
Entrances (2006)

Translation
A Leaf About To Fall: Selected Poems – İlhan Berk (2006)
Madrigals – İlhan Berk (2008)
Book of Things – İlhan Berk (2009)
İkinci Yeni: The Turkish Avant-Garde (2009)
& Silk & Love & Flame – Birhan Keskin (2010)

In Turkish
Aradaki Ses (The In-Between Voice, 2005)
Avrupa'nın Küçük Tanrıları (The Little Gods of Europe, 2007)

HEARING STILL

George Messo

Shearsman Books
Exeter

Published in the United Kingdom in 2009 by
Shearsman Books Ltd
58 Velwell Road
Exeter EX4 4LD

www.shearsman.com

ISBN 978-1-84861-022-4
First Edition

Acknowledgments
Exeter Flying Post for "Near the Village of Qana, in the Hamlet of
Khuraybah"; *Shearsman* for "Fable", "It's alright" and "Will You Ever
See New Brunswick?"

CONTENTS

for Semra

Man speaks in that he responds to language.
This responding is a hearing. It hears because it
listens to the command of stillness.

Martin Heidegger (1889–1976)

Ton silence
Parlera pour toi

Abdellatif Laâbi

Ilahi

Rising for the Fajr prayer, water's morning
coolness says "wake & go & sit before
your god. Be mindful of the candle's losing

flame. For now you are neither east nor
west, neither night shrouded nor day burning.
Wash for a god you cannot ignore".

Light will be on you like a rash. Bow down
and say: *affliction and all that I have I own.*

for Deena Linett

Answers at Dawn

I

Wake
      to wet asphalt
           glistening:
first touch
          first sun

II

Morning–
      hearts:
          your
     micro–pearls
scattered in roadside grass

III

Night
      folds
          like
a concertina:
      distant skirl of cormorants

Windstorm. Oman.

Anger makes
     you small
          useless
& therefore
     silent
shaking
     through
the bricked–
     up box
we call
     a home

while out–
     side sand
en–
     crouches
grain
     on
          grain
around our
     desert lives.

Anger
     has
no use
     for you,
small;
     this
bricked-up
     life

we count
        as home
grain
      by
           grain.

Will You Ever See New Brunswick?

There are rivers we will never fish.

Is this one of them?

You walk alone to the forest pool.

Does it know I'm coming?

Spring grilse have news from the sea.

Is it something we should know about?

There are no myths, but mystery persists.

The earth's visible gasp rises
    as mist into crisp air over water.

for Scott Andrew Christensen

Dune

Dune:
the word
you enter by, crouched
on sand

We know
nothing, and this
is all we know:

With sand
you make an hourglass
make a wall

Prophecy

after Adonis

From our thousand-year-long sleep
out of our savaged past
comes sun, no ceremony
to this place scored into our lives like a tomb
to this comatose, brutalised land
killing the sand sheik and the sheik of flies

Time grows on the plain
time withers on the plain
like a fungus

A sun, homicidal, ruinous,
rises over the bridge

Horses at a Trough

Man
he guzzles down
that dungspit mouthwash
slurps it good
his turdbreath prayers
for the god who gave it

We are up for any
comewhatmay to wet
our speechcracks
caught without a lick
out here. In heat.
Come across a plain.

Fable

A monochrome land.

           Was snow

     and there were pines:

           infant, dwarfed.

Horizons,

      you could almost touch

but never reach.

              Sky

was black or grey

              but never white.

A memory

      of what we did

              and were.

Setting Out

Wolf packs crowd the heart
there comes a time to run

but always too many paths
and knowing their length

tires us before we start
the fatal scream is bourn

within there comes a time
to let it out when bones

vibrate like tuning forks
and the body-tone's wave

trembles over forest floors
finds the wolf-heart

finds the wolf

It's Alright

Our way
to say
we glimpsed
the abyss
but its door
has closed
once more.

Breath in.
As long as
you can hold it.

Nakeeb
is going down
to the river.

Trout skins
plumb & cool
will know him.

Light,
their ever
moving chamber,
springs them
from its trap.

Nakeeb.
"ya Mustafa"
supplicants
cast their lines.

Water enters
through the mouth,
finds its cul-de-sac.

Breath out.

Bats

after Samih Al Qasim

Bats at windows
bleeding my voice
at thresholds
scratching poems
shading my path
in corners cracks
and crevices
wherever I go
on chairs
in streets
on books up
girls' tender thighs
wherever I look

…

Bats like
electronic bugs
hidden in walls

…

I'm digging
a hole
to daylight.

The Hotel Room Waits

Go!
The house is intolerable—

its warm hands
at your throat;

its rhetoric of upturned
boats, stranded,

miles inland.

Desert Plum

I

Vine–choked trellis
like lovers' wrists
entwined and inseparate:
when morning's cool blade
will cut them yet

II

Does the sleeping face
wear sadness?

Wash off September leaves
put on winter

III

Though small
still you reach

plums future-fat
bough-bending

Reading Tagore: Three Poems

Necessarily Now

i.

Poor human heart,
you say
there is no time
for looking back.

But see!
My mullet head
(glares out from here)
was always

staring back.
Scattered words
that trace
the lines

you might have been.

ii.

Living well
is like forgetting.

I used to have a farm —
fields and wooden barns,

somewhere
by a stream —
(forgotten name).

"Where's Rukmini now?"

iii.

Randomly
you pick four words
"the temple-light went dark"
which surely
says "you're here"

if not
necessarily now.

So Music Enters the World

Song is marriage
(Rabindranath Tagore)
no wind

                no rustling leaves

The Rainstorm's Hymn to Cloud

"The sun is dead!"
(Tagore again, perhaps)

Death (a word
I'd never use
and therefore
surely T, not me)

puts mouth to ear
inhales
the echoing voice.

Dream–Fear

after Adonis

Naked

        they came

ransacked

        the house

dug

        a hole

buried

        the child

and left

O My God, Who Uses Words
Like *Truth* These Days?

I'm quoting Kenny Fountain my friend
in the title of this poem when suddenly
I read in the July/August issue
of Foreign Policy John J. Mearsheimer
and Stephen M. Walt say *AIPAC* see
endnote *and many of the same neo*
conservatives who advocated attacking
Iraq are now among the chief prop
onents of using military force ag
ainst Iran and they go on to say
there's nothing improper about pro-
Israel advocates trying to influence
the Bush administration. But it is
equally legitimate for others to point
out that groups like AIPAC and
many neoconservatives have a commit
ment to Israel that shapes their
thinking about Iran and other
Middle East issues. Sooner or later
on page 59 paragraph one in his
essay entitled *An Uncivilized Argument*
Aaron Friedberg is going to say
while others cower in silence, they
[meaning Mearsheimer and Walt] *brave*
accusations of anti-semitism to speak
truth to power.
                    It's good to know eight
thousand miles from here the intellectuals
are fighting it out on our behalf.

Documents

The Middle East's a powder keg
Hamed reads
and asks what means this keg

He studies air
takes out rolls up
a cigarette (index fingers thumbs)

puts (slowly) to his lips
twists takes out & taps on teeth
and holds his match aloft unstruck

Yes
he says
a powder keg.

Near the Village of Qana, in the Hamlet of Khuraybah

i.

One Sunday
on a hillside
covered with trees
midnight crept
into our village.

It stayed forever.

ii.

Daylight
is our new blindness

we take
what is left

of our children
and go, down

to the village
of Qana.

iii.

There
we take off
their clothes.
Wash off
what dust
their hands
still hold.

They will
be clean
forever.

Wednesdays

i.

Rima, wake up!
Your weight
has put my
leg to sleep.

Ala, get up!
and wash
your hands
and feet.

Sanah, the
Fajr prayer
is tapping at
your door!

ii.

Where
are you
now, that
time & all
its muezzins
cannot wake
you from?

Rima, wake up!
Ala, get up!
Sanah, the
Fajr prayer!

iii.

Hold
the body
of Rima,
one-year-old

so
she does not fall
from you
Umm Sanah

as
she lays beside
her sister Ala
in the drawer

of a morgue
fridge in a
Beit Hanoun
hospital

Wednesday
November
eighth
2006

Aziziyah, Al Khobar

1.   The time
you read
these words
I will
have left
this tense
and moved

to any
– an other –
altogether
closer time

if
nouns
do not mis-
take my
place I'm
here (& then
I'm not)
Aziziyah
Garden Village

2.   Not all of this enough
said I would not want
again this bed again
Al Khobar dust again
Aziziyah Garden Village

3.   Up at dawn
or soon before—
he woke arose
(was woken)
climbed a minaret

but then
what thoughts
were those

enslaved
to thinking minds:
if death were not a door
but only metaphor

unlocked
ajar
swinging by a hinge

4.   Their gift
is form
& shape

yet
thoughts
can move
a form

if not
through
physical
space:

Aziziyah
Garden
Village.

A Memory of Myself

You were
then

& from
my desert-
now:

a mirage.

The Shifting Nouns Are On Us

1. A
    pool
    a
    river—
    one
    of all
    the things
    as good
    or
    better
    still
    a place
    to start
    to make
    a start
    to cast
    the lan—
    guage
    on

2. The shift-
   ing nouns
   are on them
   – those
   who wear
   this word-
   weave out-
   side in

3. Let's
   for ex-
   ample
   say you're
   wading
   in

   the ver-
   bage
   moved
   to make
   you there

   a river–
   one

4. Shade
   instan-
   tiates a
   tree &
   weight
   its rock
   or small-
   er space
   assumes
   a stone

5. Is th-
   inking
   made
   to fit
   the cage
   it's cap-
   tive in
   ?
   A land
   so very
   like a
   noun
   pretend-
   ing it's
   a
   pool
   a
   river-
   one
   of all
   the things
   as good
   or
   better
   still
   a place
   to start
   to make
   a start
   to cast
   the lan-
   guage
   in

Like Sometimes Days

I

It's the physical body
        that dreams
                and yet

to be
        unknown
be un-
        thinkable

a thought
        must leave
                its flesh.

II

Do you know yourself?
And is there space enough
around these words
to feel if questions
really are two silent
hearts or heads too
filled with answering
to hear what's said?

III

It is
sometimes
enough
to know
a thing,
its why
& when
and where.

IV

Do we know ourselves?
Or are these other ones
so much a part of each
themselves that neither
none not any one
can tell?

V

Fate
is
future
running
back
through
time.

&
dreaming
is a
temporal
thing.

VI

To think
a thought
must
peel
its flesh,
must know:
itself,

a body
yet.

Ilahi

What are you? And whose shape
is your soul in now? How
did the He of your escape
become this other you? Who

speaks through gestures you articulate?
My heart I give to you.
These are my hands; this, my fate.

Traces

after Güven Turan

Night
sea voice

heard
inertia

a breath in sleep

and waking
into darkest pitch
your lover's
stoic face

love's
shoreline flesh

To walk
in your voice

to be lost

sense is concrete
lights occlude the path
changing the broken view

leaving always
the same trace

no trace

returning
to beginnings

no beginnings

Following
night's long
rain

light
migrates to
the orb of a streetlamp

sharp
the leaf-fan

drops of light
falling into darkness

rain holding off
the more to hold on

The road passed
each morning

suddenly to stop and look

vast sky
small park

empty

missing
bench legs
pond
half-full

"copper coloured leaves"

to walk away
a blind eye turned

Then rain begins
in a garden

there is no garden
so who knows
if rain fell or not

the city's
morning dampness
under feet of sleeplessness

vanishing

Hand stretching out

to emptiness

waiting
snow will fall
without
winter's help
the bud is lifeless

hand
still in emptiness

Eyes believe
in what they see

watching
your lover undress
before a mirror

looking out to sea
in early hours
of a summer day

chiaroscuro

Quietly
I withdraw into forests

feeling and talking
coalesce

I wait for nothing

desolation

To see
a meteor shower

and wish
for nothing

The dice is thrown

no chance

each face of the dice
erased

chance

In the photograph
no one

a tree
a house

shadow of a cat
across the wall

a newspaper on the pavement
lifting off

surprising

not
surprising

On Seeing the Princess Semra
Dancing the Waterfall Mime

I

I think
they help
to hear
the fertile
leap,

wind's
random
influence
on water
falling
over rock,

the whole
brought out
in sounded
tones
as politic
as it gets

II

The theme
expressed itself
as 'long
ago gardens'
unvisited,
as 'twisting
terms' all
poetry:
difficult,
dynastic.

III

And what
you want
to say
instead:

"spring water,
origin's. end."

Flowing
in its
grammar,
just

Would Winter Call You Snow?

1.   To hear
                        if only hearing could

     the voice you're said upon

                                        say

                all of this

                            this all
                                  this

          everything

        is what it is
              because
                       of what it was

2.   And when he talks alone

                                        he talks to you

        it's true   *I do*

        this thoughtful self-filled act I wrap in you

        & hear

                        if hearing can

                your nearest sounding voice

                        you all

                                you everything

3.   And what it takes from me
                                 and out
                                      of me

            the ego-god is stilled

         I call it what you will

      but call it   *will*

                   a willingness
   to cast in silence
            stones
                 of saying

                        hearing still

for Kenny Fountain, once again

Ilahi

What night is this outside that fears
our prayer and makes your heart a place
of refuge? Its darkling tongue appears

to speak for us, to anyone who hears.
This is all we are, the smallest trace
of light, a prayer, before it disappears

Notes

Adonis: The pseudonym of Syrian poet Ali Ahmad Said Asbar, born 1930.

Aziziyah: A district of Al Khobar in the Eastern Province of Saudi Arabia.

Beit Hanoun: A city in the North-East of Gaza, Palestine. On 8 November, 2006, Israel Defence Forces shelled a row of houses, killing 19 civilians. Thirteen of the dead were of the same family.

Fajr: The first of five daily Muslim prayers.

Güven Turan: Turkish poet born near Sinop on the Black Sea in 1943.

Ilahi: A hymn or spiritual song in the Muslim tradition.

O My God,. . . : AIPAC is The American-Israel Public Affairs Committee.

Qana: A village in Southern Lebanon. On 30 July, 2006, Israeli air-strikes killed 28 people; 16 were children.

Samih Al Qasim: A Palestinian Druze poet, born in 1939.

The Shifting Nouns . . . : I had in mind W. S. Graham's poem 'Seven Letters' as a place of orientation and return.